INSPIRE AND REFLECT

INSPIRE AND REFLECT

SCARLETT NORA

CONTENTS

CHAPTER 1

Introduction

Welcome to **Inspire and Reflect: A Teacher's Guide to a Joyful School Year!** This guide is crafted for educators who are eager to further discover and refine their craft, become inspired on their journey, reflect on their experiences, and reignite their passion for teaching. Whether you're engaging with this guide as part of a book club or as a solitary reader, you'll find weekly reflection activities designed to delve deep into the book's messages and enrich your teaching practice.

This guide is not just about enhancing your teaching during the school year; it's about encouraging you to explore new content and revive areas that may have been neglected. Our hope is that you will take time to care for yourself throughout the school year, equipping yourself with the tools and passion to make a profound impact, because teachers truly do change the world.

Starting the school year with joy and optimism sets the stage for a successful and fulfilling journey. By choosing to bring joy and triumph into your professional environment, you foster a positive atmosphere that benefits both you and your students. Move forward without fear and without looking over your shoulder. Prepare yourself with positive affirmations, clear goals, and accountability practices. Embrace the tips provided to revolutionize your approach and ensure a joyful year. Understand the three steps to recalibrate your joy if it's not where you want it to be. Transform your practices and elevate your professional development to shine throughout the school year.

Setting the Tone for a Joyful School Year

It all starts with that first day back on the job. The beginning of the school year is a critical time for setting the tone for a joyful, vibrant learning environment. Whether you call it the beginning of the end, the first pathway to success, or the opening scene in the act of mastering your craft, the truth remains: the first days and weeks in the classroom are pivotal.

How we set the tone, the messages we communicate, the heart we demonstrate, and the leadership we exhibit matter immensely. Rather than starting with a list of rules and expectations or diving straight into academics, focus on teaching joy. Ignite interest and curiosity. Let these initial moments be a delightful preview of the learning to come.

When we set a tone of exuberance, whether we're new to a school and feeling uncertain, or returning to familiar territory, we create an environment where lessons and learning can thrive all year long. As we greet students for the first time, remember that it's their first time meeting us. Set an atmosphere of confidence, energy, humor, and care. Launch the relationship between student and teacher with a celebration, understanding that who we are and how we interact all year long are greatly influenced by how we begin.

CHAPTER 2

Building a Positive Classroom Culture

One of the primary concerns for many beginning teachers is managing student behavior. Questions like, "How am I going to get students to do what they're supposed to do?" and "How am I going to deal with students who disrupt my class?" are common. While these are important considerations, classroom management involves much more than rules, procedures, and discipline. At its core, effective classroom management is about creating a social environment where students feel valued, respected, and eager to engage in learning—not just for the sake of high academic achievement, but because the environment is inherently supportive and designed for success.

Practical Tips for Building Classroom Culture:

- **Sit at Each Desk**: Experience your classroom from your students' perspectives. How does it feel to sit at each desk? Is there enough room to write and read? Can a student comfortably share a book with a peer? What can they see or not see from each spot in the room?

- **Harmony and Friendship**: Foster an environment where students look out for each other. If a student is having a bad day, encourage classmates to offer support. A simple "Is there something you want to talk about?" can make a significant difference. Encourage students to communicate their whereabouts and ensure no one feels isolated.

Creating a Safe and Inclusive Environment

Whether you are a new teacher or have years of experience, establishing a positive classroom culture is vitally important. This not only helps students feel comfortable engaging in higher levels of thinking and problem-solving, but it also lays the foundation for strong relationships. As the adult in the classroom, you set the stage for the classroom culture from day one. One of the first and most important things you must ensure is that each and every student feels safe.

In a safe environment, all students can take risks, not just those deemed "smart." Creating an inclusive environment is also crucial. When you effectively prepare for inclusion, everything else falls into place. Remember, creating a safe and inclusive classroom is an ongoing process. Inclusion is not a box to be checked off; it is an aspect of the classroom that should be continually reflected upon and improved. Here are several steps to create a safe and inclusive environment:

- **Start on Day One**: Develop procedures and routines for all activities right from the start.
- **Role-Play Expectations**: Clearly demonstrate and role-play what you expect to see in your classroom.
- **Get to Know Your Students**: Invest time in truly understanding each student's unique needs and backgrounds.

- **Personalize Learning**: Tailor your teaching strategies to meet individual learning styles and preferences.
- **Reflect on Discipline Plans**: End your discipline strategies with problem-solving and reflection to promote understanding and growth.
- **Continually Assess Practices**: Regularly evaluate and improve your inclusive practices.
- **Encourage Empathy**: Foster empathy and understanding among students to create a supportive community.

CHAPTER 3

Effective Communication with Students and Parents

Good communication is at the heart of building trust and rapport with your students and their families. For younger children, this often includes their direct teacher and the school's administration; for older students and those with more extensive involvement in their schools, it will also involve their coaches, sponsors, and other mentors. Effective communication helps avoid falling into an often divisive "us" versus "them" mentality. Starting your relationship from a perspective of goodwill and working toward shared outcomes makes those outcomes more likely to happen.

Practical Steps for Effective Communication:

1. **Open the Lines of Communication Early**: Begin with welcome letters that include all your contact information (phone, email, address) and the best times to reach you. Ask parents for the same information and the best times to contact them. Two-way communication starts at the beginning of your relationship and should happen regularly. Instead of setting up formal meetings just for discussing concerns or problems, ensure there are regular opportunities for open communication

to address any potential issues or needs proactively. If regular opportunities for communication are not currently part of your strategy, make a plan to integrate them in a manageable way.

Building Trust and Rapport

It is well-researched and supported by countless testimonies that the statements we make to open a school year set the tone for how we will communicate, collaborate, and teach our students. During the opening days of school, three central purposes of adult speech emerge:

1. **Getting to Know Learners and Sharing Ourselves**: Establishing a connection with students by sharing who we are and learning about them.
2. **Building Trust**: Creating an environment where students feel safe and valued.
3. **Inspiring Students with Creative Wonder and Unlimited Potential**: Encouraging students to see the limitless possibilities in their learning journey.

Reflect on these criteria before moving to classroom practices that have been shaped by numerous exemplary veteran teachers. Before your summer training, consider how you will communicate with your students to build these important relationships.

Parent Onboarding and Scheduling Considerations

The first days of meeting families are crucial for building trust and rapport. Parent onboarding should have two primary goals: developing trust and fostering a sense of community within your classroom and school. Consider sharing information about the growth their children will make over the school year. By sharing your knowledge of what the students will learn, the procedures they will acquire, and the progress they will make, you begin to form that important bond of trust from the start. Show an energizing level of enthusiasm for the new school year.

To further build a sense of community, enlist the help of parents by asking them to write a letter about their child. These letters, which offer insights from the parents' perspectives, are invaluable. Many parents enjoy doing this, and their responses can provide significant insights that are worth their weight in gold.

CHAPTER 4

Innovative Teaching Strategies for Engagement

Enthusiastic educators constantly explore new teaching strategies to spark students' creativity and love of learning. The most effective methods inspire learners and motivate them to actively participate in high-quality instruction. This section outlines several diverse approaches, highlighting interactive teaching tips that value affective, creative, kinesthetic, and musical strengths. What happens when educators incorporate these innovative strategies?

Research shows that students who engage in role-playing perform better in "imaginative open-ended" measures of creative thinking. Even more crucial for classroom order and instruction, these methodologies increase depth of knowledge and critical-thinking skills, promote a positive approach to learning, improve reasoning, and counteract school difficulties. Creative educators design projects that align with content, processes, and products, making the process last long enough to ensure creative problem solving occurs. They increase the challenge at each step, provide an element of mystery and surprise, and establish public audiences. These inventive teaching strategies help inspire and maintain the attention necessary for learners to aim high.

Utilizing Technology in the Classroom

Innovative Teaching Strategies: Utilizing Technology in the Classroom

Many students will agree that teaching and learning with technology, when done right, can be excellent. One of the most effective ways to use digital technologies is by introducing new resources or platforms for homework, class activities, or assessments. Rather than forcing technology to fit into the existing curriculum, consider adopting a new teaching approach that seamlessly integrates digital tools. When teachers embrace technology and make it an accessible and integral part of the classroom, they can engage students in meaningful ways. Share your favorite new apps, educational or non-educational, that can truly engage any student.

Practical Tips for Utilizing Technology:

- **Interactive Platforms**: Utilize platforms like Google Classroom or Microsoft Teams to streamline communication, assignments, and feedback. These platforms allow students to engage in collaborative projects and discussions in real-time.
- **Educational Apps**: Introduce educational apps like Kahoot! for interactive quizzes or Duolingo for language learning. These apps make learning fun and gamified, increasing student engagement.
- **Virtual Reality (VR) and Augmented Reality (AR)**: Use VR and AR to create immersive learning experiences. For example, Google Expeditions allows students to take virtual field trips around the world, enhancing their understanding of different cultures and environments.
- **Flipped Classroom Model**: Implement a flipped classroom model where students watch lecture videos at home and engage in hands-on activities in class. This model leverages tech-

nology to maximize classroom interaction and application of knowledge.

- **Online Discussion Boards**: Use online discussion boards, such as those on Google Hangouts or Edmodo, to facilitate discussions outside the classroom. These platforms encourage students to express their thoughts and engage in debates on various topics.

Teachers can extend learning through technology by choosing the right resources or content uploaded on a platform, making the transition to new tools for homework seamless for students. Services like InstaEDU, a tutoring platform, show students how to learn quickly and efficiently using the internet. Digital resources, such as educational games and apps, transform learning from merely reading content to engaging with it. It can be as simple as having an online discussion board via Google Hangout, where students participate in live chats about recent activities.

CHAPTER 5

Promoting Student Well-Being and Mental Health

Addressing the well-being of students is of utmost importance. Schools are not only places for education but also spaces where children are nurtured emotionally, physically, and socially in a holistic way. Every student deserves a successful education that provides opportunities for better academic achievement, reduces risk-prone behaviors, and helps them become healthy and productive individuals in the future. Educational institutions committed to students' mental and emotional well-being by promoting student welfare, health, and safety play a crucial role. Creating a supportive and secure school environment is both an essential goal of education and an effective strategy to assist successful student education.

As teachers, having strategies and practices in your classroom plan to nurture each child's comprehensive growth is vital. Whether focusing on mentally friendly infrastructure, promoting good relationships, developing empathy, teaching gratitude, or incorporating Question Formulation Techniques (QFT), leaders today urge teachers to implement these strategies daily. Students who regularly learn and integrate these exercises develop socially and emotionally. Developing appropriate classroom teaching procedures ensures that all students feel accepted and respected. Teachers focus on increasing the social-emotional and moral welfare of each student through hands-on physical activity and positive community-building routines—efforts that help create a peaceful world.

Implementing Mindfulness Practices

In our quest to promote student well-being, we are implementing mindfulness practices throughout our school to elevate the power of reflective thinking and create positive school culture experiences. By starting with staff, who may feel stressed, anxious, and overwhelmed, we plant the seeds of mindful reflections during beginning-of-year staff meetings, allowing the time needed to grow emotional well-being and reflective growth.

"When it comes to education, the unique positive impacts mindfulness has are in neutralizing negative conditioning, cultivating a new understanding of our emotions, and shifting some of the unconscious and reactive patterns of behavior to more wise and reflective actions," says mindfulness-based stress reduction facilitator Michelle DuVal.

The brain science of mindfulness highlights its importance in biochemistry, showing immediate and well-documented positive increases in attention abilities and compassion toward oneself and others. Recent studies provide preliminary evidence that adolescents' depressive symptoms and happy-brain activity can change following mindful training. Over time, mindfulness reduces internal struggles, leading to beneficial improvements in brain connectivity. Mindfulness practices positively influence the emotional regulation system of children's brains, enhancing their overall well-being. Offering mindful moments expresses care at a neurological level, helping students "feel thoughts and name them."

CHAPTER 6

Celebrating Diversity and Inclusion

This chapter will explore the uniqueness of diversity and inclusion and why it's crucial for every educational setting. The spirit of inclusiveness will permeate this guide as we suggest ways to create a safe and positive classroom community where the voices and experiences of people of all races, national origins, genders, and sexual orientations are valued and seen as important. Recognizing and celebrating diversity through a variety of texts, children's literature, and non-literary texts will be a primary method of acknowledgment. The strength derived from children working and playing together in a diverse learning community will be our focus. Most importantly, we aim to advance the feeling of belonging that we want to foster in our students.

The Importance of Belonging

Belonging goes beyond mere inclusion. In a class, students might feel invited to sit at the lunch table and join in the games, but they may still feel they don't truly fit in. Educators dedicated to building a diverse and inclusive classroom understand the importance of providing validation that sends the message, "I am glad you are here, and I want to know more about you." Culturally responsive educators aim to create a learning environment where students know they are accepted and feel comfortable sharing their experiences and contributing to classroom discussions.

Fostering Empathy

Teachers who already have, or want to develop, a curriculum they feel good about—or are at least interested in trying—have another road to cultivating the feeling of belonging that will bring us all together: cultivating empathy within the understanding of all students. When students can feel what someone else is feeling, they have taken a significant step toward understanding that person's humanity. Empathy is an emotional skill that can be taught and practiced in many ways. By intentionally teaching empathy, we move powerfully toward creating a community of young people who overwhelmingly understand and value the experiences of others. Honoring the multitude of experiences that every one of our students brings to our classrooms is both responsive and loving and will bring our students together.

Culturally Responsive Teaching

The sixth thematic unit of **Inspire and Reflect** focuses on diversity and inclusion, particularly on culturally responsive teaching. This concept can take many forms, from incorporating the arts and traditions of Black, Indigenous, and people of color to shifting the way we respond to negative behaviors. Here you'll find a variety of strategies for practicing culturally responsive teaching both in and out of the classroom. These resources are intended for you to adapt to fit the needs of you and your students. Incorporate these practices when they align with your goals. If your goals aren't represented here, feel free to share your ideas or needs in your reflections.

As more strategies are collected, this section will grow. Aim for one to three paragraphs per strategy, annotating each with descriptions and additional links to media or other resources. Culturally responsive teaching goes beyond inclusive practices. The activities included here are part of a larger process of critically examining our curriculum and pedagogy, our relationships with each other and our students, our classrooms, and our school community. We must continually keep our minds open and adaptable while cultivating respect for the skills, experiences, and traditions of all students, educators, paraprofessionals, staff, and administrators in our schools.

CHAPTER 7

Professional Growth and Development

The word **inspire** comes from the Latin word meaning "to breathe into." It suggests the sacred nature of teaching and learning; as teachers, we breathe life, hope, and possibility into the lives of children. Although we may feel stretched thin or weary, few callings are higher than educating young people. Amid our hard work, we find incredible joy, satisfaction, and yes, stories. Our profession is built on the knowledge that we can always learn more about how children grow and develop, the subjects we study, the art of teaching and learning, and the world in which we all live. Professional growth and development are lifelong pursuits for educators.

Teachers who excel thrive on classroom diversity, employing various activities, lesson plans, and assessment tools suitable for individual interests and learning styles. Highly skilled teachers engage in self-reflection and are deeply committed to lifelong learning. In other words, the best teachers never stop developing and honing their skill sets. Professional teaching draws heavily upon the teachers' own process of learning—both the teacher and the students are learners in the learning environment.

Pedagogical knowledge and reflective practice must be consistently developed and nurtured to ensure engagement, equity, inclusion, and high-quality learning. The teacher's personal growth should be consistently nurtured through reflection in the profession, strategic engagement with professional growth and development, and the ability to critically engage with pedagogical practices that increasingly focus on both academic and socially rich learning tasks. Reflective practice and continuous professional growth and development are vital components of an actively engaged, committed teacher, essential for creating and maintaining an engaging, inclusive, and caring classroom and school community.

Reflective Practices for Continuous Improvement

Cultivating a culture of collaboration and using an inquiry approach to uncover needs and develop solutions allows everyone to share in the experience and ensuing pride. However, changes in behavior or practice are not always immediately evident; they require time to establish baseline standards. It is essential for individuals to develop a clearer understanding of their work practices and the impact these have. Each of us must engage in a process of self-reflection and self-assessment as part of a continuous improvement process.

Reflective practices, combined with other organizational change mechanisms such as collaborative teams or goals agreed upon in team performance management, align with performance management theory. Reflective practices help individuals define what they will set goals about, which is one of their key roles. Direct feedback, particularly constructive feedback, is crucial in reflective practice, as it helps individuals understand the extent to which their behavior, practices, or outcomes are appropriate. Feedback provides another reference point for self-assessment.

Reflective practice isn't just about looking back at what worked or didn't work; it's about creating a framework for thinking critically about teaching practices and student learning. Here are several strategies to integrate reflective practices into your professional development:

1. **Journaling**: Keep a reflective journal where you can jot down thoughts, challenges, and successes from your teaching day. This can help identify patterns over time and foster deeper insights into your teaching methods.
2. **Peer Observations**: Arrange for regular peer observations where colleagues can provide constructive feedback on your teaching practices. This can offer fresh perspectives and highlight areas for improvement.
3. **Professional Learning Communities (PLCs)**: Join or form a PLC with other educators to discuss strategies, share resources, and collaborate on problem-solving. Regular meetings can provide continuous support and inspiration.
4. **Professional Development Workshops**: Attend workshops and conferences to stay updated on the latest educational research and teaching strategies. Engaging in these events can reinvigorate your teaching practice and provide new ideas to implement in your classroom.
5. **Student Feedback**: Gather feedback from your students about their learning experiences. This can provide valuable insights into their needs and how your teaching can better support their growth.

Reflective practices are a cornerstone of professional growth and development. By continuously engaging in these practices, teachers can ensure they are meeting the needs of their students while also nurturing their personal and professional growth.

CHAPTER 8

Collaborating with Colleagues and Building a Suppo

Teachers are silhouette thinkers: they have a grand knack for inspiring others by conjuring breathtaking visions, yet on most days, they search for inspiration likewise. The allure of the educator is the practitioner, the dogged analyst who looks for the noble in the nitty-gritty of children and uses this to create an emerging future. The work of teaching is inherently collaborative. Educators must feel part of a larger community with shared goals. Schools must be primary communities, and when educators feel a deep sense of connection, their work improves and burnout is vastly reduced.

The educator who constantly wishes for students to arrive with no excuses is cutting off a frayed shirttail. No one in education shows up with a blank slate. Every student comes with prior experiences of all kinds and varying amounts of social capital. Educating students is a matter of shared responsibility and ongoing effort. Like Isaac Newton said, "If I have seen further, it is only by standing on the shoulders of giants." If I am now an educator and a successful one, it is only by standing on the shoulders of the educators who have gone before me. We are nothing outside of a community. We all only are because of those who have gone before us.

Teamwork and Shared Goals

Good teamwork, as any football coach can attest, leads to great things. Athletic teams and corporate groups alike work best when everyone knows where they want to go and collaborates to get there. You might come from diverse places and have different skills, but your attitudes and perspectives balance one another, and one thing unites you: a common goal. As teachers, we too can bond, energetically aligning to let professionalism meet purpose. Expertise will support (and, at times, question) different expertise, and in this way we can achieve broader outcomes for the good of all. We work in a school filled with resources, willing and able students, and supportive parents—all ready to share in the pursuit of educational excellence.

Embracing a Collaborative Network

Enthusiastically embracing a collaborative network, we will find support in times of need, helping one another express myriad opinions and balance decisions. Families will see that their children are attending a strong, supportive, and committed school where excellence is an outcome and change is a constant. Resources will flow through our programs, into our rooms, for those who need it most, and this will be reflected in the faces of our children. Our school will be recognized as reflecting the very best of humanity. In unity, we hold the power of force and far-reaching influence. As the Mexican proverb says: Many grains of sand can make the mountain. Individually we rust, together we shine. In our unity, we are a beacon of determination for change and a true sense of community. In power, we unite. In hope, we shine. Together, we hold the brilliance of what the future will bring. We can.

CHAPTER 9

Managing Stress and Avoiding Burnout

Every teacher deals with stress, and many burn out at some point. My experience tells me that when we make small, consistent healthy choices daily, we feel better, are more resilient, and can be better teachers. Below are several strategies to consider incorporating into your school setting to inspire well-being among your staff. Remember to first consider your staff's needs.

Ideas for Well-Being

1. **Create a Sense of Community**: Become a mentor or get a mentor. New teachers need a cheerleader, a sounding board, or a friend as they begin their teaching careers. This greatly decreases social isolation. Start an early career program in the school setting where students in education can coach adults and staff. This creates a cozy, supportive circle and is joyful for all.

2. **Incorporate Physical Activity**: Try yoga, Pilates, or simply stretch your muscles. You could even have a stretch break during a faculty meeting to relieve tension.

3. **Practice Mindfulness**: Train yourself to think peacefully. Close your eyes and be still for five minutes. Negative forces can overwhelm you if you're not able to deeply breathe in and out and clear your mind.

4. **Develop a Teaching Mantra**: Create a teaching mantra or natural ally phrase. Maybe it's an acronym like "Slow, Calm, Connect," or a chant about respect such as "Role models on three."

5. **Reflect on Your Successes**: In a journal, record three positive things from your day or three positive things your students did. Research suggests this practice incubates problem-solving, creativity, and gratitude. At your next faculty meeting, discuss some of these positive moments.

6. **Focus on Wellness**: Achieve optimal wellness by making small health-conscious choices, like drinking a smoothie with greens and blueberries. Feel entitled to do something good for yourself.

7. **Prioritize Self-Care**: Taking care of yourself reflects how you feel about yourself. Educators who consider self-care a necessity, not a luxury, remain optimistic and energetic. They embrace stress and focus on what can be changed to make things work. This internal resilience increases their longevity in the profession. Identify what brings out the best in you and give yourself permission to take care of those things.

Managing Stress

In your school, be the coach. Remain optimistic and focus on what you can change to improve what isn't working. Inside every stentorian rant or inane directive are potent bits of useful information.

1. **Create Boundaries**: When you're off duty, disconnect from work and devote yourself to personal time. The most difficult aspect of teaching isn't stress itself, but that we rarely give ourselves permission to be stressed. Accept that you will have good days and not-so-good days.

2. **Develop Physical Resiliency**: Every morning is your morning. Make choices today that are right for you. The indomitable spirit survives the longest.

3. **Cultivate Natural Intelligence**: Believe that you can fix issues in a few days and treat your body as you would a precious baby.

4. **Understand Stress Hormones**: Educate yourself about cortisol, the famous "stress hormone." Resistance to burnout depends on managing bad moods and anger. Recognize if stress triggers profound shifts within you.

5. **Recognize Stress Signs**: Make a list of your stress signs and be willing to make deliberate changes when you notice them.

6. **Control Your Thoughts**: While we can't control the world around us, we can control our thoughts because they create our feelings. Establish an identity surrounded by resilience, knowing that regardless of what happens, you'll survive. The assignments may change, but with a teaching plan and a few actionable items, stress dissipates.

Educators cannot care for others unless they primarily acknowledge that they need care themselves. This power is what educators like you use to turn lessons around, providing a healthier system to enhance both teacher and student well-being.

Self-Care Strategies for Educators
Reflective Teaching Practices

Join Dr. Elena Aguilar on August 17 for the session "Reflective Teaching Practices: A Cheat Sheet for Joy," part of the free online event. Sign up here.

Overview

The list of stressors for teachers and school leaders is ever-increasing. From students experiencing digital burnout to those dealing with the mental health effects of the pandemic, educators are feeling stressed, overwhelmed, and burnt out. While many look out for the well-being of their students and families, not all are doing the same for themselves. This session will highlight self-care strategies that educators can implement to ward off or relieve stress.

During stressful times, the easiest response is often to focus more and work harder. However, much at school remains beyond the control of teachers and leaders, so a proactive approach to well-being is vital. Self-care practices are crucial for overall health; educators, whether in person or virtual, continue to struggle with balancing classroom demands and personal care. According to the Lancet journal, over 183 countries identify addressing mental health and emotional well-being as top priorities for supporting educators. The journal lists a range of strategies for promoting mental health that includes self-care practices. This session will explore stress and well-being within the Social and Emotional Learning (SEL) framework, focusing on key areas such as nutrition, exercise, and time off for personal care.

CHAPTER 10

Fostering Creativity and Innovation in the Classro

Inspire and Reflect: A Teacher's Guide to a Joyful School Year was created to focus on the social-emotional realm and allow teachers to apply the philosophy of engaging both head and heart before the year begins. Together, we will support adults in our environments to better support their students, allowing them to shine. A guide to best practices will be shared next.

Fostering Creativity and Innovation: Embracing Joy from the First Hello, Releasing the Glue of Perfection in the Classroom, Ten Ways to Augment Student Voice and Choice for Amplifying Learning Through Creativity.

Success in learning is about so much more than mastering facts and skills. It also requires acquiring the attitudes and habits of mind that support deep, creative, and innovative thinking. Too often, we tell kids to think outside the box but then don't give them the tools or opportunities to innovate and create inside the box. Many of us place high value on creative and innovative thinking but lack experience and have not engaged in opportunities to practice these skills, either as students or adults.

Encouraging student expression and creativity can be messy, requiring trade-offs, reframing of classroom roles, and innovation for all, including educators. Once the passion for learning takes over the classroom, true learning happens.

Encouraging Student Voice and Choice

When we talk about creativity and innovation—which are the same thing in many respects—student choice and voice come up time and time again. The primary reason is that creativity and innovation can't happen in an environment void of choice and voice. It's not enough to simply allow voice and choice; we should actively encourage students to express themselves in ways that are authentic and valuable. By helping students make connections between who they are as individuals and the content they are studying, we make school relevant. We challenge kids to think about the world around them, the possibilities we have as human beings, and big issues.

In a classroom dedicated to creativity and innovation, we foster an environment where students are safe to put their ideas "out there" without fear of criticism and ridicule. When kids want to take risks and take the road less traveled, achievement happens, and kids care more deeply. Reflect on those goals you set for yourself. How are they tied to offering students voice and choice in your classroom? When we see students every day but can't see ourselves in them, it leaves us disconnected, and their "education" is devoid of meaning. Value what makes a child special, reach out to connect, and build relationships. That's the true key to education, and that's a skill that never becomes outdated.

Practical Strategies for Fostering Creativity and Innovation

1. **Project-Based Learning (PBL)**: Implement PBL where students work on projects over extended periods, integrating

multiple subject areas. This approach encourages students to use creativity to solve real-world problems.

2. **Design Thinking**: Introduce design thinking processes to help students understand the stages of innovation—from empathy and ideation to prototyping and testing.

3. **Maker Spaces**: Create maker spaces in your classroom where students can use various materials and tools to build, experiment, and invent. This hands-on approach stimulates creativity and critical thinking.

4. **Collaborative Learning**: Encourage collaborative learning where students work in groups to brainstorm, solve problems, and create projects. Collaboration fosters diverse perspectives and innovation.

5. **Art Integration**: Integrate art into various subjects to allow students to express their understanding creatively. Art can be a powerful medium for innovation and exploration.

6. **Choice Boards**: Use choice boards that provide students with options on how they want to learn a concept or demonstrate their understanding. This autonomy boosts engagement and creativity.

7. **Inquiry-Based Learning**: Adopt inquiry-based learning where students ask questions, conduct research, and present their findings. This approach nurtures curiosity and independent thinking.

8. **Reflective Practices**: Incorporate reflective practices where students regularly reflect on their learning experiences, challenges, and successes. Reflection enhances self-awareness and continuous improvement.

9. **Gamification**: Use gamification techniques to make learning fun and engaging. Gamification encourages creativity through game-based learning activities and rewards.

10. **Technology Integration**: Leverage technology to create interactive and multimedia-rich learning experiences. Digital tools and platforms can enhance creativity and innovation in the classroom.

CHAPTER 11

Assessment and Feedback Strategies for Growth

Reflective Question: Are you employing assessment and feedback in a manner supportive of the growth and development of every student?

Assessment and feedback generate response and reflection: The use of assessment and feedback drives focus in learning. The types of assessment and feedback in which we choose to engage shape the learning culture and climate of our spaces. Formative assessment allows students to utilize prior learning to make a connection to a new concept or skill and transfer that application to new learning. Our growth and development, corrections, and adjustments based on formative assessment strategies can deepen commitment and application; it goes beyond simple memory or recall. The feedback provided following a formative assessment strategy should result in self-assessment, self-reflection, and questions for further learning. If we, as educators, use assessment or quizzes as a mere record of knowledge, our feedback often reinforces that this particular bit of schooling is done. In these instances, students are finished when testing has concluded, putting a stopping point on learning merely to complete a task. Change assessment from right/wrong to learning potential, by involving the students in the process on an ongoing basis.

Formative assessment techniques sharpen focus and empower problem-solving through:

- **Strategic Questioning**: Routine use of refined feedback.
- **Student Data Notebooking**: Allow students to track their own progress.
- **Math Intervention during Math Instruction**: Immediate correction and support.
- **Culture of Precision through Math Talk**: Developing accuracy and depth in mathematical conversations.
- **Daily Math Fluency Practices**: Ensuring consistent practice of key skills.
- **Student-Selected Formative Assessments**: Engaging students in their own learning reviews.
- **Conferring through Writing and Spelling Workshops**: Personalized feedback sessions.
- **Pendleton's Loupe in Physical Education**: Observational assessment tools.
- **Early Childhood Instructional Rounds**: Peer observation and feedback.
- **Fountas and Pinnell LLI (Leveled Literacy Intervention)**: Targeted reading interventions.
- **Seed Writing**: Initial writing exercises that grow through revision.
- **Climate Walks**: Assessing the learning environment for inclusivity and effectiveness.

Formative Assessment Techniques

It's important in any course to gauge the progress and understanding of your students. Unlike summative assessments, the goal of formative assessments should be more about providing feedback and guidance on understanding as opposed to simply rating performance. There are numerous effective ways to implement formative assessments as our classrooms grow, diversify, and modernize.

Techniques for Formative Assessment:

1. **Exit Tickets**:
   - **Description**: Quick assessments students complete at the end of a class to show their grasp of the content.
   - **Implementation**: These can be tech-based (using programs like Google Forms) or done on index cards or sticky notes.
   - **Benefits**: Provides a snapshot of understanding, highlights areas of confusion, and offers immediate feedback.

2. **Tech-Based Quizzes**:
   - **Description**: Utilize online quizzes that provide instant feedback.
   - **Implementation**: Use tools that show which questions were missed and indicate spatial understanding.
   - **Benefits**: Allows for immediate correction and can be revisited before summative assessments to check for improvement.

3. **Peer Assessments**:
   - **Description**: Students assess each other's work using clear criteria.
   - **Implementation**: Establish guidelines and model effective feedback.

- ◦ **Benefits**: Encourages critical thinking and self-reflection among students.

4. **Self-Assessments**:
    - ◦ **Description**: Students evaluate their own learning and progress.
    - ◦ **Implementation**: Provide self-assessment checklists and reflection prompts.
    - ◦ **Benefits**: Promotes self-awareness and responsibility for learning.

5. **Interactive Notebooks**:
    - ◦ **Description**: Students maintain notebooks where they record their learning, reflections, and assessments.
    - ◦ **Implementation**: Use sections for notes, practice problems, and reflection.
    - ◦ **Benefits**: Integrates learning and reflection, making it easier to track progress.

6. **Learning Journals**:
    - ◦ **Description**: Students keep a journal documenting their learning journey.
    - ◦ **Implementation**: Encourage regular entries reflecting on lessons and progress.
    - ◦ **Benefits**: Develops metacognitive skills and deepens understanding.

CHAPTER 12

Promoting a Growth Mindset and Resilience

In school, the more we encourage a growth mindset—a belief that we can make our brains grow—the more risk-taking, problem-solving, effort, and insights we are likely to see. Spend time at the start of the year, and periodically throughout, contrasting fixed mindset thoughts with growth mindset thoughts. It's essential to use your own words with students to provide examples they can connect to.

Resilience can be thought of as accepting challenges. It is the ability to perceive challenges as manageable, ensuring one does not feel overwhelmed. Moreover, resilience is the capacity to carry on, rather than collapse, when things become difficult or take an unexpected turn. A resilience framework suggests that resilience can be developed by focusing on identifiable factors at the level of the individual, family, community, and culture. Adopting this framework in school reminds us to consider all the factors that can make a child more or less vulnerable.

Creating a Joyful School Year

Promoting a resilience-developmentally supportive school culture involves finding ways to help students develop resilience, which is beneficial for several reasons. It can enhance emotional well-being, foster a positive view and anticipation of learning, encourage a willingness to try, and persevere despite setbacks. Ultimately, it helps pupils achieve and, in a genuine sense, be successful. Developing a positive attitude towards learning can enhance a child's chances in initial education, lifelong learning, the workplace, and life in general.

Encouraging a Positive Attitude Towards Challenges

Although challenging experiences can sometimes feel frustrating, remember that you have the power to change your attitude and perspective. A positive attitude will help you focus on the gifts and opportunities within the obstacle. We must help students believe that if they rise to a challenge, they are likely to succeed. Facing a challenge can be a positive experience, and when things are tough and on the brink of failure, remind them: "This is where learning really happens."

Strategies for Encouraging a Positive Attitude:

1. **Contrast Fixed vs. Growth Mindset:**
   - Spend time discussing and contrasting fixed mindset thoughts with growth mindset thoughts. Use relatable examples to illustrate the differences.
2. **Model Positive Attitudes:**
   - As educators, reflect on the language and feedback given to students. Do you encourage a positive attitude towards challenges? The tone of the classroom reflects the attitudes of the teachers.
3. **Share Failures and Challenges:**
   - Encourage students to share their failures, challenges, and turning points. Reflect on these moments together to foster a supportive classroom environment.
4. **Reflect on Struggles:**

- ○ Ask students to think of a time when they struggled the most and what advice they would give to themselves or others in that situation.

5. **Develop Classroom Culture**:
   - ○ Think about your classroom culture, and if it's not where it needs to be, spend time considering how to bring about change. A supportive classroom culture helps students organically internalize the idea that hard work, persistence, and resilience are the secrets to success.

By instilling a belief in success resulting from hard work and a growth mindset, we enhance students' resilience and determination—two skills vital for facing the challenges of adulthood.

CHAPTER 13

Engaging Families and the Community in Education

Inspire and Reflect: A Teacher's Guide to a Joyful School Year is a manual for educators to help maintain a positive mindset and increase joy, energy, and vitality in their teaching and personal lives. This book comprises 12 chapters, one for each month of the school year, aiming to improve the joy and positivity of educators at all levels, from the classroom to the district, who use their abilities to help shape future generations. The central tenet of this book is that when educators are full of joyful energy and engaged in their professions, they emit a secret energy that, in a kind of magic, is picked up by their students, who start to believe in themselves.

One way to ensure that students come to school feeling connected, engaged, and respected is to create an educational village that emphasizes partnerships and collaborations between the schools, homes, and communities that serve children. Below are some better ways to rethink our stance on engaging families and communities and broaden our definition of what is possible when families, schools, and communities create strong relationships with the best interest of children in mind. When educators and family members partner to support student growth, it doubles the number of adults looking out for each child's needs. Engaging military families, transitioning families, and families negatively impacted by societal norms cements trust between home and school. Focusing on partnerships enriches the lives of all stakeholders, making each role more meaningful and impactful.

Parent Involvement Strategies

Family and community engagement are the foundation for a successful teaching career. Teachers whose students' families are involved in their school careers experience less burnout, have more positive attitudes toward their jobs, seek parental input in their policymaking and problem-solving efforts, and look for ways to engage the community in their school-building activities. However, getting parents involved can be challenging. Students may tell their parents they are old enough to handle school issues on their own.

In my experience, engaging parents effectively involves seeing them as allies. For example, I spoke with Amy Castill, an assistant principal at Nuclearly Middle School, about engaging parents for my 2004 book, "The Homework Myth." Castill emphasized that teachers should view parents as valuable partners who know their children better than anyone else at school. She invited parents for a ten-minute talk about their child's strengths, which helped to build trust and understanding.

Here are some strategies to enhance parent involvement:

1. **Create Open Communication Channels**:
    - Establish regular communication with parents through newsletters, emails, and parent-teacher conferences. Make sure they feel welcome to share their thoughts and concerns.
2. **Host Family Nights and Workshops**:

- Organize events where parents and students can participate in fun, educational activities together. Workshops on supporting learning at home can also be beneficial.

3. **Volunteer Opportunities**:
   - Encourage parents to volunteer in the classroom or at school events. This involvement helps them feel connected to their child's education and the school community.

4. **Parent Surveys and Feedback**:
   - Regularly ask for parent feedback on school policies and practices. Use this input to make improvements and show parents that their opinions are valued.

5. **Cultural Celebrations**:
   - Celebrate the diverse cultures of your student body by hosting cultural nights or incorporating cultural lessons into the curriculum. This fosters inclusivity and respect.

6. **Parent Advisory Committees**:
   - Form committees where parents can collaborate with school staff to discuss and address school-related issues. This builds a sense of shared responsibility and partnership.

7. **Home Visits**:
   - Conduct home visits to build stronger relationships with families. These visits show parents that teachers care about their child's well-being beyond the classroom.

8. **Community Partnerships**:
   - Partner with local businesses and organizations to provide resources and support for families. This can in-

clude after-school programs, tutoring, and access to social services.

Engaging families and the community in education creates a supportive and enriching environment for students. By fostering strong partnerships, we can enhance student growth and well-being, making education a collaborative and joyful journey for all.

CHAPTER 14

Creating Memorable Learning Experiences

The best learning is the kind that students remember and value long after they have left our classrooms. Memorable learning experiences can be the catalyst for long-term change. Beyond making the classroom experience truly meaningful for each child, such activities capture the imagination, a prerequisite for better retention of information. Field trips or visits from interesting guests can grab hold of our imagination and make us want to know more. This is the perfect frame of mind for igniting students' curiosity. Often, a great field trip or powerful visitor makes learning come to life for our students, possibly for the first time, amidst the mundane experiences associated with tests and standardization.

As educators, we can apply our internal push for meaning and experiential reward to our own practices. If we learn and grow by doing, our students can develop in much the same way.

Field Trips and Hands-On Activities

Field trips are phenomenal opportunities for learning engagement. Whether conducted during or before a unit of study, they provide students with memorable learning experiences, serve as anticipatory sets, offer accessible background knowledge, or supplement post-study classroom reflection and discussion. To best facilitate learning, field trip planning must first meet school or district requirements and support specific educational goals.

In a mathematics workshop, field trips give students real-world applications of mathematical concepts, allow them to experience abstract concepts concretely, or help them understand the value of such concepts.

We have long recognized the enjoyment music brings. Music can transport us back in time and evoke strong emotions. Mickey, an educator with a goal of "inspiring musical adventures," would take his classes on "trips" to the music room to explore, listen, reflect, and share. This inspired him to embrace community lessons, where all students would have string or percussion lessons in music class rotation. These "musical adventures" created vivid memories and a stronger connection to learning. Back in the classroom, students could write and talk about their experiences, incorporating writing, sharing, and listening standards into a "real world" activity.

Experiential learning opportunities create a stronger connection to the content. When planning field trips and hands-on activities, consider the following strategies:

1. **Align with Curriculum Goals**:
    ◦ Ensure that field trips and hands-on activities align with your educational goals and curriculum standards. This helps make the experiences meaningful and relevant.
2. **Pre-Trip Preparation**:
    ◦ Prepare students for the field trip by discussing what they will see and do. Provide background information and set learning objectives to maximize their engagement.

3. **Interactive Activities**:
   - Plan interactive activities during the field trip to keep students engaged. Encourage them to ask questions, take notes, and participate in hands-on tasks.
4. **Post-Trip Reflection**:
   - After the field trip, facilitate discussions and reflections on what students learned. Incorporate writing assignments, presentations, or creative projects to solidify their understanding.
5. **Community Involvement**:
   - Involve the community by inviting guest speakers, local artists, or professionals to share their expertise. This brings real-world connections into the classroom and enhances the learning experience.
6. **Integrating Technology**:
   - Use technology to enhance field trips and hands-on activities. Virtual field trips, online research, and digital storytelling can provide additional layers of engagement and learning.

Creating memorable learning experiences requires thoughtful planning and a focus on engaging students' imaginations. By incorporating field trips and hands-on activities, we can make learning come to life and leave a lasting impact on our students.

CHAPTER 15

Empowering Student Leadership and Agency

One of the key markers of a brain-friendly community is that it has high levels of student leadership and agency. It is so important that our students lead initiatives or projects that matter to them. Not only do they carry out the necessary, respectful, collaborative conversations and decisions, but they also gain permission and agency to organize and run these projects. Here are some ideas on how to shape an environment rich with student voice and choice, starting with some examples in action.

- **EFPSA Group, ENOHE**: This group gives students, parents, and professionals in higher education the opportunity to converse about their lived experiences with mental health. Students are completely in charge of moderating these sessions. They will soon be involved in designing the final online toolkit and will run the final discussion at the next conference.
- **ESEII Partners NVOK in the Netherlands**: This initiative has student-led projects aimed at preparing students to become profession-ready social entrepreneurs. High school stu-

dents reach out to primary school children, giving lessons on programming, cooking, film editing, and VJing.

Student-Led Initiatives and Projects

Shifting the spotlight from what the teacher is doing to catalyzing what students are contributing invites agency and leadership. Here are some ways students have led and contributed to their school communities:

- **K-5 Thrifting for the Earth School**: Students have advocated for a school focused on sustainable practices.
- **School-Based Charity**: Students have started charities within their schools to address various social issues.
- **Pythagorean-Lobbing Action during Math Games**: Students have donned professional basketball jerseys and engaged in math games, making learning fun and interactive.
- **Spontaneous Performances**: Students occasionally burst into performances, such as the Cup Song or singing the Greek Sun/Stand song, fostering a lively and engaging school culture.

Creating spaces of homage to teachers, inspirations, and mentors, while finding smiles and joy alongside community, is the sustenance many educators seek in their work. It is an act of reflection and joy, part and parcel of daily learning.

Engaging in student-led projects is both fun and a commitment to shared pedagogical values. Through agency and leadership, students build capacity, confidence, acceptance, and self-responsibility. Projects are joyfully and intentionally messy, dedicated to the process rather than the product. This approach fosters experiences, ownership, reflection, passion, and friendships, allowing everyone to grow into something better.

ownership, reflection, passion, and friendships, allowing everyone to grow into something better.

CHAPTER 16

The Role of Creativity and Play in Learning

Creativity and play are just as important to learning as reading and writing, yet in recent years they seem to have been given short shrift in our schools. The push for rote memorization and a one-size-fits-all curriculum can short-circuit children's natural curiosity and their love for learning. Incorporating play-based learning into a curriculum helps in numerous ways. It can feed creativity, spark imagination, and establish important neurological connections that will last a lifetime. It becomes a whole-brain learning activity, which means it's both fun and growth-nurturing at the same time.

To state the purpose of play in your own words, the strategies for integrating play into your educational game plan should be clear and thoughtful. Once you've started giving play a proper role in the classroom, it becomes easier to see how purposeful and organized it can be. Whether through games of strategy, word play, or active playtime, it is essential to allow students to stretch their wings and make their own decisions. Unstructured playtime is also crucial. The experience of play is beneficial for students in many ways, from learning practical skills to understanding the more abstract realization that goals are good things. It is fundamentally beneficial to use play in a classroom setting—if only we can disconnect the term "play" from "wasting time." Empowering and enlightening classroom teachers is the first step to achieving this.

Incorporating Play-Based Learning

Just let them play. Simple, right? It's not a new idea; old ideas simply work. There is a tendency in education to avoid play in schools, yet play is inherently linked to learning. Children are remarkably smart. They invented childhood, and if we pay attention to them, we might learn a thing or two. Research supports the idea that play is a child's work, as coined by the beloved Fred Rogers. A theory called constructivism suggests that children learn through doing, through hands-on activities. This is why literature circles, project-based learning, labs (yes, even for something as abstract as grammar), and hands-on manipulatives tend to work—they are about the action. Engage students in the work. Why wouldn't we allow them to learn through play and invented worlds in a similar way? Children deserve to be children. The play-based learning philosophy encourages play and the sharing of imaginative thinking to build a stronger learning community.

Later, I will share some simple ways to incorporate a play-based philosophy and tools to bring this world to life. Catherine L'Ecuyer also talks about the research behind joy, laughter, and happiness in learning. This kind of happiness is integrated into educational development. It is harder and sharper than the fleeting high of a compliment; it is resistant to unhappiness. Happy learning can dispel the moans of impending work. A joyful classroom fosters a want to learn. It is simply more fun to learn.

Strategies for Incorporating Play-Based Learning

1. **Literature Circles**:

- Allow students to discuss books in small groups, fostering a love for reading and collaborative learning.

2. **Project-Based Learning**:
   - Engage students in projects that require critical thinking and problem-solving, connecting their learning to real-world issues.

3. **Hands-On Activities**:
   - Use manipulatives in subjects like math and science to help students grasp complex concepts through tactile learning.

4. **Creative Arts**:
   - Integrate art, music, and drama into the curriculum to allow students to express themselves creatively and emotionally.

5. **Play Centers**:
   - Set up different play centers in the classroom where students can choose their activities, from building blocks to role-playing.

6. **Outdoor Learning**:
   - Take learning outside with activities that explore nature and physical play, connecting students to their environment.

7. **Game-Based Learning**:
   - Use educational games that reinforce academic skills while making learning fun and interactive.

8. **Imaginative Play**:
   - Encourage students to create their own stories and scenarios, developing language and social skills.

9. **Joyful Classroom Environment**:
   - Create an atmosphere that celebrates curiosity, laughter, and discovery, making learning a joyful journey.

10. **Teacher Modeling**:
   - Model a playful and curious attitude towards learning, showing students that it's okay to explore and make mistakes.

Incorporating play into the classroom helps students develop holistically, fostering creativity, problem-solving, and a lifelong love for learning.

CHAPTER 17

Cultivating a Love for Reading and Literature

One of the most rewarding, albeit challenging, aspects of teaching is to bring literature to life, inspire students to become lifelong readers, and create a vibrant reading culture within your classroom and school community. Several factors come into play when attempting to cultivate a love for reading and promote a passion for literature. These include acknowledging that students' reading preferences may not always match our own and incorporating multimodal, multimedia, creative, and differentiated instructional strategies.

We must also encourage and model literature-affirming work, engage students in lifelong patterns of consumption and production of texts in multiple forms, consider not just interest but readiness and challenge in literature selection, and emphasize a love for literature over a fear of reading. These grounded and practical readings for deep thinking and influencing classroom practice are essential and inspiring for pre-service and in-service teachers, scholars of literacy education, and students of literate arts and textual teaching circles at all levels. If we can grow readers, we are also growing writers. Literacy is the heart of all learning and teaching, and all teachers are literacy teachers.

Thorough literacy skills, understanding, appreciation, enjoyment, and production of signed systems (including the visually printed ones) can help us all follow our passions and build a happy and productive future. As teachers and parents, we have a unique opportunity to inspire children to read and help the next generation appreciate the value of reading in their lives. Our classrooms and communities can become legions of enthusiastic, committed, and reflective readers for a lifetime. When we raise reader children, we change the world.

Promoting a Reading Culture

Students who are proficient readers not only develop literacy skills but also gain knowledge and interest in the world around them. Because of the many benefits of reading, most teachers hope to impart a love of reading in students. As teachers plan for the new school year, there are many things educators can do to create a happy and informative environment that shapes individuals. They can provide a variety of books that students will enjoy reading and offer opportunities for students to read both individually and in group settings.

It's not enough to expose learners to various kinds of books to promote a love of reading. It's also crucial to educate students on literature, how to enjoy it, and tie it into their own lives. In addition to simple comprehension, when learners are asked to reflect on texts and consider questions like "what would you have done in this situation," the literary experience becomes more meaningful to them. Furthermore, educators must show students that they are part of a community of readers.

Here are some strategies to promote a reading culture:

1. **Provide a Variety of Books**:
   - Offer a diverse range of books that cater to different interests and reading levels. This ensures that every student can find something they enjoy.
2. **Create Reading Opportunities**:
   - Set aside time for independent reading and group reading sessions. Encourage students to discuss what they're reading with their peers.
3. **Incorporate Multimedia**:
   - Use audiobooks, e-books, and visual aids to complement traditional reading. This makes reading accessible to all learners and caters to different learning styles.
4. **Host Book Talks and Reviews**:
   - Allow students to present their favorite books at the school library or leave reviews on a class website. This promotes a sense of community and shared literary experience.
5. **Connect Literature to Life**:
   - Encourage students to draw connections between the literature they read and their own lives. Reflecting on how they relate to characters and situations makes reading more personal and engaging.
6. **Praise and Endorse Contributions**:
   - Regularly praise and endorse students' positive contributions to the reading community. Publicly or privately offering rewards can motivate a love for reading.
7. **Organize Reading Challenges**:
   - Create reading challenges and competitions to make reading fun and goal-oriented. Reward students for meeting their reading goals.
8. **Model Reading Behavior**:

- ◦ Share your own reading experiences with students. Let them see you reading and discussing books you're passionate about.

9. **Establish a Reading-Friendly Environment**:
   - ◦ Design a comfortable and inviting reading space in your classroom where students can enjoy their books without distractions.

10. **Engage Families**:
    - ◦ Involve families in the reading process by encouraging them to read with their children at home and participate in school reading events.

By implementing these strategies, educators can cultivate a love for reading and literature, creating a community of lifelong readers.

CHAPTER 18

Promoting Global Citizenship and Social Responsibi

Having students develop into global citizens who are aware of local and global issues is a crucial part of education. In recent years, pressures such as economic and technological changes, politics, and an ethic of global competition have encouraged schools to take more seriously the task of developing mature and responsible citizens of the local community and the world. Teachers must promote increased global awareness and engage students in becoming empathetic individuals committed to addressing local and global challenges. To have an impact on the world, one first has to understand the world. While the world may seem too complex for teachers to develop a global citizen mindset, there are actions one can take to further this goal.

Many young people today describe themselves and their generation as apathetic in a society where images of violence and suffering are more common than ever and no longer shock or spur individuals to take action. The best way to confirm or challenge these claims is to talk to young people openly and honestly about their attitudes toward the global society in which they live. Social responsibility has several advantages for students. Compared with less involved counterparts, teenagers who become socially involved undertake more causes and contribute more time to serving others. Civic action can also benefit the psychological and social health of the person who performs it.

Service Learning Projects

The teachings of global citizenship and social responsibility are explicitly addressed in this chapter through the incorporation of service learning projects. Service learning is a broad concept, and with educators' obsession with defining key terms, overthinking, or general resistance as the first reaction, the conceptual understanding may take a while. Nevertheless, learning through service is what educators have been practicing for centuries as they build character. Community service projects are seen as a few hours of students' lives in which they work for the common good. They may be motivated by a sense of empathy, compassion, ability "to give back," a desire to help, or a "need to do something" as a response to a tragic event. Whole-school projects or programs by various grade levels often appeal to schools. These projects are usually organized by teachers; if involving partner organizations, teachers tend to rely on their support to get students to service sites.

Looking beyond handouts, organize some service activities to help students integrate content, demonstrate learning, and engage in service that is meaningful to them using their passions, talents, and interests as they become the change needed in today's world. In this way, students can learn and demonstrate that social action is a necessary part of achieving United Nations' Sustainable Development Goals and becoming more globally-minded citizens. Service learning is more explicit in purpose. It implies a relationship between the service and what one learns. Becoming personally aware of the connection motivates students to see themselves as stakeholders in society who can make a contribution through personal action. Helping the less fortunate and contributing to improving conditions in one's own neighborhood enhance a student's sense of empathy and obligation to assist. Becoming aware of personal responsibility promotes an active or practical "knowing what" sense of service or citizenship more effectively. These students can become our new workers in organizations, volunteer at social service agencies, advocate on social issues, and, hopefully, educate the next generation of children to be empathetic world citizens.

Navigating Challenges and Overcoming Obstacles

Whether it is coping with a natural disaster that changes lives and livelihoods in a community, or trying to provide quality remote instruction for students, educators encounter tough and often unexpected professional challenges. As difficult as conditions might be in our schools and communities, fostering resilience as a response can empower both educators and students to initiate change within themselves and in the broader context of their school lives. Many researchers have explored building resilience in educational settings, realizing that championing change and overcoming challenges play a critical role in students' psychosocial development.

Providing a meaningful space where educators can discuss challenges, problem-solve how to support themselves, and use the problems to inform their practice is critical. Many educational researchers understand the value of offering emotional first aid to enable transformative discussions. To create a safe environment where individuals can explore changes that matter to students, educators, and the community, and learn from such investigations, it's essential to foster an atmosphere where challenges and changes are discussed openly, rather than avoided. For a reflective process to flourish, talking about failure and how to overcome it can be a powerful motivator.

Resilience in the Face of Adversity

Overcoming adversity depends on our perceived consequences when faced with challenges. Developing resilience is a way to avoid the paralyzing effect of adversity. We must reject the belief that we have no other choices. One option is to quit, to run away as fast as we can. The other is to prepare for a battle, to move forward with the knowledge that scars are souvenirs we never lose. We can be comfortable and more confident knowing that we have faced challenges and won. Perseverance and determination are bolstered by understanding that when our resolve is tested, we and our students and colleagues are being prepared for something greater. Find a way to look ahead. Embrace Nemo's mindset: "Just keep swimming."

Given English language learners, students with special needs, and those who exhibit challenging behaviors, the classroom may sometimes seem like an uphill battle. When the going gets tough or when adversity seems to loom around every corner, resilience, persistence, commitment, and perseverance are just a few critical survival responses to the myriad of challenges that may confront teachers. Where do I find the power to teach even on days when I feel like disappearing from the face of the earth forever? It lies in perspectives, philosophies, mentors, and strategies that promote empowerment. A change of attitude and goals is an essential part of our ability to move forward. Unfortunately, adversity most often finds additional ways to counteract our deepest drives or reverses our efforts to move on to something greater. We are encouraged to adopt a mindset that sees joy as something inside us that we cultivate to maintain a balance between personal well-being and our work.

Strategies for Developing Resilience

1. **Create Supportive Networks**:
    ◦ Establish professional learning communities (PLCs) where educators can share experiences and support each other. Mentorship programs can also provide guidance and encouragement.
2. **Focus on Self-Care**:
    ◦ Encourage self-care practices such as regular exercise, mindfulness, and taking breaks. Educators need to prioritize their well-being to be effective in their roles.
3. **Reflective Practice**:
    ◦ Engage in reflective practices, such as journaling or peer observations, to identify areas of strength and growth. Reflecting on challenges and successes can build resilience over time.
4. **Set Realistic Goals**:
    ◦ Set achievable goals that are challenging but attainable. Celebrate small victories and progress along the way to maintain motivation.
5. **Professional Development**:
    ◦ Participate in professional development opportunities that focus on building resilience, classroom management, and student engagement. Staying informed and equipped with new strategies can empower educators to navigate challenges effectively.
6. **Cultivate a Positive Mindset**:
    ◦ Promote a growth mindset in both educators and students. Emphasize the importance of effort, learning from mistakes, and viewing challenges as opportunities for growth.
7. **Community Involvement**:

- Engage with the broader community to build a network of support. Collaborate with parents, local organizations, and other stakeholders to address challenges collectively.

8. **Adopt Flexible Approaches**:
   - Be open to adapting and trying new strategies when faced with challenges. Flexibility and creativity can lead to innovative solutions.

By adopting these strategies, educators can build resilience and empower their students to face challenges with confidence and determination. Embracing adversity as a learning opportunity can lead to personal and professional growth, creating a positive and supportive educational environment.

CHAPTER 20

Conclusion

Revisiting our themes from the introduction, ponder the following questions: What sort of teacher do you want to be? What sort of classroom do you want to have? Take a moment to let these questions simmer, because deciding to have an amazing classroom is the first step towards creating one. And who says it has to be a bad year anyway? Let's avoid the stress that comes with resistant students and instead welcome the energy and dynamism they bring. I am excited about the personalization I will witness this year, and the unique ways my students will find meaning in their learning. It is an abstract, artistic task that will draw me in completely.

Lastly, remember to revisit the first part of this book. Many people do not have the conversations or reflections presented within, with many tools to use as the year progresses. Even discussing these matters with your peers can be enlightening. This journey has been significant. But here we are, finishing with the same message: the tools for a peaceful life are the same tools that bring a satisfying school year. I am avoiding the stressed-out teacher archetype with enthusiasm because no time is a good time to consciously choose to be unsatisfied with life. Instead, let's aim to draw in satisfaction by having a fulfilling school year and thank each step of the way for the early opportunities.

Reflecting on a Joyful School Year

What are your favorite memories from joyful learning experiences this year, either as an educator or a student? As you record your reflections about this year, consider the insights you've gained from your successes and turnarounds. Time draws to a close on the books you've finished with your students, each completed task another chapter you've helped bring to a close for them. Reflecting on this year, what story has this draft of time helped you write on your own heart? Your reflection strengthens your intrinsic motivation, helping you anticipate the journey ahead.

You have grown just as much as your learners during this joyful school year. We depend on the experiences we've had to grow. We try new approaches—sometimes they succeed, and occasionally, we miss the mark. But reflecting on these experiences helps us learn. We benefit both from the affirmations that come from our reflections and the opportunities to do better when we brave the learning curve again. You won't be starting from scratch when you walk into your classroom. You'll bring all your prior experience with you, and you have a lot to offer! You've just single-handedly tackled your first year and changed the trajectory of your classroom and your students' lives. Reflecting on your intentionality and the values you hold will affirm that you have indeed grown as a professional.